WHAT OTHERS ARE SAYING

There are truths to be found in what are normally thought of as ordinary things. Mrs. Harris has a special talent for finding such truths, presenting them to the reader in a compelling and humorous way in her book, *Israel: My Journey and Reflections on My Life*. For example, "*We talked and laughed for a bit and then put my suitcase on the scale. Guess what? My bag was overweight, so I had to take my peanut M&M's out. Now these are my favorite snacks, so I'll have to come up with something else to take out.*"

Seeing the world through Father's eyes was the most outstanding feature of this woman's story that captured my heart, including our Lord in *every* detail of her preparation for this trip and during the trip as well. Here's one example as what she sees when most of us would not take notice. "*The day is beginning to dawn, it's just a little cool, and the heavy dew on the ground looks like shining diamonds on the grass.*" How Mrs. Harris views the world around her, whether it be her *family*, her *buddy Annie*, or *the long lines of waiting* are nothing more than encouraging. Seeing life through what I call the Jesus Specs or Jesus Glasses is how it can be described.

Mrs. Harris is the embodiment of Philippians 4:8, *"Fix your thoughts on what is true and good and right. Think about things that are pure and lovely, and dwell on the fine, good things in others. Think about all you can praise God for and be glad about."*

Telling you—after reading this encouraging and compelling story, you'll be looking for your Jesus Glasses as well, because it makes for a beautiful world to live in.

Thanks, Mrs. Harris, for sharing your story. Everyone who calls themselves a Christian should read this.

—Cesar and Gloria Ochoa
Poway, California

To read *Israel: My Journey and Reflections on My Life* is to see the full picture, the divine, and the miraculous in our lives. You will be inspired and challenged to allow God to be involved in every aspect of your life. I highly recommend this reading for anyone who desires to see as God sees in our every circumstance.

Sharing the personal and practical experiences of everyday life to prepare for her trip to Israel, in her book, *Israel: My Journey and Reflections on My Life,* Mrs. Harris exposes the wonderful characteristics of our Lord, and how He orders her steps along with others to make this awesome trip possible. God is in the house!

In the fascinating adventure of pursuing intimate friendship with the only One who can totally fulfill us, Mrs. Harris makes it clear that the price of serving is high, but the privilege and rewards are higher.

In *Israel: My Journey and Reflections on My Life,* courage, discipline, endurance, and love are the character qualities expressed through this wonderful (then 74 years old) woman who simply loves God. Through her temptations (peanut M&M's), troubles, and challenges, she manages to pursue the will of her Lord to go to Israel. You'll be blessed from her experiences as Mrs. Harris draws parallel lessons to what God wants from each of us to do and be: His coworkers.

—Cesar and Gloria Ochoa
Poway, California

We shared this trip with Sister Frances, so we can see that this book is a delightful recollection of what she experienced. It will bring back tender memories for all of you who have traveled to Israel. If you have not yet been to this great land, this book will give you a firsthand account of the special experiences that will be in store for you.

She narrates her personal experiences in the Holy Land. Many of the sites she encountered were significant places concerning the history of Israel, but also there are places relating to the life of Jesus while on this earth. She describes both of these, and blended with all of this; she relates of her engaging the people of Israel who live in the land of these special places. She tells of a parade she marched in through downtown Jerusalem, with the streets rimmed with the Jewish residents, thanking the Christians for showing support for the nation of Israel.

There is one other set of special areas to take the time to absorb, which are the places that tell of the saga of the formation of the nation of Israel, from the Holocaust Museum to the British Immigration camps and the triumph of the Western Wall, which now serves as the symbol that secures Jerusalem as the capital city.

The Lord then adds His comfort by showing Sister Frances how this blessing was one of many she received from the Lord.

This is a fitting way to crown her experiences she wrote about by honoring the One who blessed her with those experiences.

Thank you, Sister Frances, for this contribution.

—Paul Dillinger
Escondido, California

This book has special meaning, as a portion was read to my wife, Frances Tapscott, by Frances Harris (my Frances's namesake) on the last weekend of my wife's life. The story of her journey to Israel was ministered to my wife as she was completing her journey on this plane.

As I read the opening of Frances's book, I was marveling at how God moves in our lives as He prepares us for our own journey. It is such a joy to see how God lays out His plans for our life while we sometimes try to tell him of our plans. I am reminded by the quip "want to make God laugh? Tell Him what your plans are!"

Frances Harris is a woman who has been blessed with the knowledge that we are all in good hands when we acknowledge and then follow His direction. Be blessed as you read this book about this one journey God placed her on and how it will continue to bless others during their journeys.

—Jim Tapscott
Escondido, California

Sent to the author's daughter Crystal Ochoa:

I just finished your mom's book! Loved it! She is such a gem in our Lord's crown! It was awesome seeing Israel through her eyes and hearing her stories of life, death, love, family, serving the Lord, travel, and discovery too! I love her precious heart for our Lord and for all her children and grandchildren! She is truly a mother in Israel (the kingdom). Thanks for sharing it with me, and be sure to tell her that I loved reading it!

Blessings,
Claudia Maddux
The Connection Church, Poway, California

Absolutely amazing, smart, and inspiring. A remarkable journey of faith, hope, and love.

—Rev. Dale Brackins, former senior pastor of
Panorama Full Gospel Foursquare Church

Israel

MY JOURNEY AND
REFLECTIONS ON MY LIFE

FRANCES L. HARRIS

Israel

MY JOURNEY AND
REFLECTIONS ON MY LIFE

TATE PUBLISHING
AND ENTERPRISES, LLC

Published by Tate Publishing & Enterprises, LLC
127 E. Trade Center Terrace | Mustang, Oklahoma 73064 USA
1.888.361.9473 | www.tatepublishing.com

Tate Publishing is committed to excellence in the publishing industry. The company reflects the philosophy established by the founders, based on Psalm 68:11,
"The Lord gave the word and great was the company of those who published it."

Book design copyright © 2014 by Tate Publishing, LLC. All rights reserved.
Cover design by Gian Philipp Rufin
Interior design by Mary Jean Archival

Published in the United States of America

ISBN: 978-1-63268-891-0
1. Religion / Christian Life / General
2. Biography & Autobiography / Religious
14.08.14

DEDICATION

This book is lovingly dedicated to God the Father, and Jesus Christ my Savior who has saved, blessed, and kept me all these years with such love and grace. I can only imagine, without Him, this book would be impossible.

To Edmond, my husband of fifty-seven years, who was and still is the love of my life, a man of prayer, a wonderful pastor, and an awesome father.

To our precious daughters and their husbands, and our son and his wife, our grandchildren, great-grandchildren, and great-great-grandchildren who have always shown us much love and respect, and who so lovingly and kindly helped me on my journey to Israel and in completing this book.

Last, but not least, I'd like to thank my church family and friends who are too numerous to name, but have a great place in my heart and life, and who bring so much joy to me.

Thank you all!

—Queen Mother

INTRODUCTION

"For out of Zion shall go forth the law and the word of the Lord from Jerusalem."

—Isaiah 2:3 (KJV)

According to the Talmud, "Eternity means Jerusalem." This idea is certainly not lost on those who have journeyed to Israel and visited the eternal city. A common expression for travelers who have experienced the mystery, spirituality, history, and grandeur of the Holy Land is "I felt like I found my home." This little spot on Earth, roughly the size of New Jersey, has captured the hearts of millions across the ages, from kings and rulers vying for the land, to those who simply wanted to walk the patriarch's land or see where their Messiah had taught, healed the sick, proclaimed the good news to the poor, and ultimately died and rose again.

What follows is the extraordinary account (expressed in her own words) of one Christian saint miraculously making *her* way to Israel at the ripe age of seventy-four years young. Born in Texas, Frances Anderson moved around quite a bit as a youngster, eventually finding her way to the tiny town of Patoka, Indiana. Married at the youthful age of sixteen to the tall and handsome Edmond Harris, Frances had decided early on to follow the Lord, turning her back on the world and following Jesus with her whole heart.

She came into the church of God in Christ in 1950 after marrying Edmond Harris. She was saved and filled with the Holy Ghost with evidence of speaking in tongues at the district's Sunday school night meeting, under the leadership of Overseer William, Sunday school superintendent; J. C. Pitt; Pastor B. T. Borroum; district Sunday school superintendent, Mother Emma McFarland; and state Big Sister Sunshine Susie Borroum. She was in the church before Bishop O. Freeman came to Indiana. Before that, they had overseers. Lucille Mattox, a friend of mine who babysat and took care of my children, had a brother named Worth, who was an overseer, one of the only two overseers she knew. From then on, there were only Bishops in Indiana.

Her life had been a chock-full of challenges and blessings—from raising eight children on a small household budget, co-pastoring with Edmond for twenty-nine years, mentoring countless young and old Christians, having eighteen grandchildren, to being a general blessing in her small farming community. Through it all, Frances was always grateful, thanking the Lord for his provision and, as she would say, "keeping me in my right mind."

On December 27, 2007, Frances's life took a dramatic turn as Edmond's life on Earth ended, his soul being called to be with the Lord as his body succumbed to cancer. At her husband's death, Frances had no idea that within ten months her feet would walk the streets of Jerusalem and the shores of the Galilee—the very places where the Jesus that she and Edmond had preached about and shared with others had walked two thousand years before.

TRIP BEGINS
OCTOBER 7, 2008

This trip actually began about twelve or thirteen weeks before departure. Walter Carter, a man of God and a family friend of ours, had a dream in which he was resting on his couch, saying to the Lord, "I sure would like to go to Israel and see the Holy Land."

The Lord responded, "Send Sister Frances."

"Wow! Sister Frances!" Walter repeated in the dream.

What Walter didn't know, was just a few weeks prior to his dream, my daughter Ruth Ann (the sixth of my eight children) had called and told me that their family (her husband, Ken, and sons, Kuri, Dylan, and Harrison) were going to Israel in the fall. I thought that was good, even wonderful for them.

Ken and Ruth Ann had traveled to Africa previously so this wouldn't be a big deal for them to travel so far. I told some of my family about their upcoming trip but never mentioned a word to Brother Walter.

In June, Ruth Ann and the boys came home to work and help out on the family farm. On Father's Day, several of our family members were at Bunker Hill Church, the church Edmond and I had pastored for twenty-nine years before his passing. This would be the first Father's Day without him with us. Brother Walter comes to me at church and says he wants to talk to Ruth Ann. I said okay and just left it at that. Then the ball begins to roll. Walter told Ruth Ann about a dream he had had and that he wanted to send me to the Holy Land.

Ruth Ann said to Walter, "Holy Land? What Holy Land?" It was such a surprise for her to hear. It knocked her right off her feet.

Walter repeated, "The Holy Land in Israel!"

She excitedly told him, "My Lord! Walter, Ken and I are taking the boys there for the Feast of Tabernacles this fall."

"My gosh!" Walter exclaimed. "Well, that is the confirmation I need that the Lord wants Sister Frances to go. What will it take to send your mom?"

Keep in mind that I don't know the details of Walter and Ruth Ann's conversation. Also, I didn't have any desire to go to Israel—even after hearing that my daughter would be going. Despite that, Ruth Ann and Walter began to plot and plan a trip for me! I've never even been out of the United

States and folks are working on getting me to go to Israel. I find out later that they considered not telling me about the trip until all the arrangements had been made. That would not have been a good idea. They would have been surprised by my response.

Over the next few days, Ruth Ann began talking to me about the trip and all the details. My initial response was that I'm not sure I should go. Maybe if it had happened fifty years earlier, then I would have accepted the trip with gladness. This reminded me of when Edmond began his ministry years ago teaching the Young People Willing Workers (YPWW) in Patoka, Indiana. He said to me that it would be great to one day go to the Holy Land. That was impossible at the time, so we forgot all about it. Ruth Ann suggested to me to just think about it, but we would have to start working on getting my passport in case I decided to make the trip.

The passport is a story all in itself. Because I didn't have a birth certificate, the passport office wanted other documentation to verify that I was a US citizen. Keep in mind that I've been living in the same community for more than sixty years of paying taxes, living, serving the community, sending my children to the local schools, and preaching in the churches. But the passport office needed more proof that I existed. So Ruth Ann with help from my fifth child, Susie (who lives in LA), started to work on the situation. They called schools I attended and local court houses. They looked up stuff on the internet and talked to anyone who could share a little light on my birth and what my name and parents' name were. Ruth Ann was asking me what I could remember from my childhood, but keep in mind that I'm seventy-four, and turning back the clock at this point is not easy. My mother wasn't married, so I wasn't sure what name she would have used at the hospital when I was born. In those days, parents didn't talk about private matters and children didn't ask.

As a child, I recall moving around a lot with my mother who, most of the time, was a single parent. I'm guessing, when I was born, mother was using her maiden name, Harrison, so that became my name. Later, she married a Crawford, so that became my name until I went to live with my mother's sister, Wilma, who had the same name as my father—so I became an Anderson! I just "adopted" these names along the way. Mind you that none of them were on paper or legal. I was just jumping on a tree like a tree frog looking for stability.

So the search then continued for information to get my passport. At one point, Ruth Ann asked, "Mother, where did you go to school?"

"Well, here and there." Not only did I take on names, but Mother would take us to live almost anywhere. I tried to stay as long as the family let me be as good as could be, and worked very hard so they wouldn't mind me being there. My little brother (Odell) would go wherever mother moved us but not me; I didn't like moving.

One story I told Ruth Ann about school was at Palmer Turner in Tennessee, living with my mother's brother Jeff, and Carrie Harrison. We were in class and a picture of President Roosevelt fell off the wall and the teacher was so upset. "Catch it, catch it!" she cried out, but no one could, and it fell and broke. At that time, an "old wives' tale" we had been taught was that if you let a picture of someone fall and break, that person would die. It wasn't long after this that President Roosevelt did die, not from the falling picture of course. It was his time to go.

Ruth Ann was able to contact the school district in Tennessee in the hopes of finding some records of me being there. The passport office had told my daughter that getting enough other information such as school records would be very important since I didn't have a birth certificate. Unfortunately, the school district in Tennessee told us that a fire had destroyed all the school records at Palmer Turner from my time being there.

So the search continued to Evansville, Princeton, and Patoka—all places where I had went to school looking for any evidence.

In all this, it was like I wasn't here, but thank the Lord I'm here with a husband of fifty-seven years, eight beautiful children, eighteen grandchildren, sixteen great-grandchildren, wonderful son-in-laws, and an awesome daughter-in law. Did I mention that with all the moving around and having children at a young age—I was sixteen when my first daughter, Linda, was born—that I wasn't able to complete high school.

But the Lord had a plan in that as well—helping me get my GED at the age of forty-five!

Eventually, we were able to gather enough information to get my passport. Ruth Ann took me to the post office where we filled out all the paperwork, and I had my picture taken. They told us it would take a week to ten days for the passport to show up, but it came early which surprised us.

So now I'm thinking about the trip. Because Ruth Ann's family will be flying from California to New York, I'm going to have to travel by myself from Indianapolis to New York before I meet up with them. I'm not too happy about that, even though I knew it was a wonderful gift and would be an awesome trip.

Let me tell you about my gift giver, Brother Walter. You may be thinking why he would want to do such a thing as send me to Israel. Walter's life is a miracle as well. He grew up an orphan boy with not much coming his way in life. The help that he did receive let him know there was a better way of life than living in foster homes—where there wasn't a lot of loving or caring. When Walter came in contact with Jesus, he then began to truly understand loving, giving, and obeying the voice of God. I'm not the only person who has been on the receiving end of Walter obeying God to bless others. It truly is more blessed to give than to receive, and Walter truly had received from God.

As I was thinking about the trip, I wondered how of all times this was happening. I thought about who will travel with me. I knew I would be with my daughter and her family, but it would be nice to have a travel partner.

When Ruth Ann's husband, Ken, found out that I would be going, he took it as a sign that he should invite his mother as well. Sister Annie immediately said yes. So now the "cheese is getting more binding" for me. Annie and I both love the Lord and like each other very much.

Oh yes, a little interesting note about Sister Annie and myself. We were in church service many years ago, and she prayed for a good Christian girl for her son, Ken. You must see this picture to believe it. Over twenty years ago, I am black, just praying and praising the Lord; and she is white with red hair doing the same. The Lord answered our prayers. Ruth Ann and Ken have been married over twenty years with three wonderful sons. All is well when the Lord is in the plans, or better still, when He makes the plan. So both Annie and I were on our way to Israel. I talked to Annie and she said, "What have I agreed to?"

"Well, we're off!" I said.

Our son Ken is so faithful. He is sending us literature and tapes of Hebrew. The more I read, the more I'm interested in getting clothes lined up. The whole family and friends got involved—they are talking about the trip more than me. I'm still quiet though. My head was involved, but my heart was not quite there. Time was moving on, and the children were trying to bring me into the twenty-first century. They got me a new digital camera, and what a joke that was trying to keep it out of my eye and focus at the same time. It took several tries. Now you just aim, click, smile, and you have a picture. The iPod—whatever that means—came next. My miracle twin daughters (Crystal and Christina, numbers seven and eight of our children) put songs and conversational Hebrew on the iPod, so I could just walk and listen. My wonderful twin daughters were quite the surprise to our family many years ago. At the age of forty-three, I was thinking I was going through menopause but that wasn't the case. I gave birth to not one but two beautiful baby girls. It was a shock to my system and life, but I wouldn't trade them for anything now! Two years later at age forty-five, I received my GED, so this was quite a time in my life.

Everyone was now in the act and participating in helping to get me ready for the trip. Every day, there were numerous telephone calls from many people, children, grandchildren, and friends all asking me, "How are you feeling about the trip?" Well, the answer was "I am getting there." Several weeks have passed and the word was truly getting around now. I'm getting cards with spending money, new walking shoes, etc. One special card came from the daughter of a lady that my husband and I had helped over thirty years ago. We were driving home one evening from a church service in Evansville, Indiana, when we saw a lady with her young daughters walking along the side of the road. Their car had broken down, and they had no place to go. We took them to our house to stay. They stayed for quite some time. They had no idea that I have children too and that one of my daughters had kidney disease and ran on dialysis weekly. To show her gratitude, the mother learned how to hook our daughter onto the machines. It was such a blessing to us at that time. Someone had told Julie, the woman's oldest daughter that I was going to Israel. The card she sent had a money order for $500 in it! What a beautiful return gift to me. These gifts just kept coming—large and small—from many different people.

One of my grandchildren, Tamara, said I needed a new suitcase. "Grandma, you need to get one you can pull." Imagine that. My husband and I have traveled with the old suitcase and it did just fine keeping the clothes inside. Oh well, I'm in the twenty-first century now. So my grandchildren came together and purchased me suitcases that actually rolled!

At this point (about 4 weeks prior to leaving), I am still not excited but had started telling a few friends that I know God must have a wonderful ending to this story as well as a beautiful spiritual gift for me.

Another gift that was given to me came from a son and daughter of ours in the gospel, William and his wife, Sandra McClendon. These two beautiful people came to visit often and enjoyed talking to my husband. Brother McClendon was called into the ministry at the church we pastored. He spoke at Edmond's homegoing service. He was also the last preacher to honor Edmond at his twenty-ninth appreciation, stating, "This is your time." We were so appreciative of them and their friendship over the years. They sent some money to me a little early for the trip, but I ended up giving that money away to others around me who were in need. I told this story to one of my daughters and said, "I guess I'll have to call them to get some more!" But I didn't.

One of the things I wanted to do on this trip is to take a gift to Israel. I decided to pack fifty sets of toothbrushes and toothpaste, however I didn't have any idea how much room this would take up in my suitcase. The gift was to be given to ICEJ (International Christian Embassy in Jerusalem) who would then bless the Sudanese refugees in Israel. Because they were taking up so much space, I mailed them to my daughter in California who then got them sent to the ICEJ. Well, I would be able to take a few treats to snack on—how about that!

By this time, I'm getting excited about the trip. Let me give you a little insight into why. In September of '07 I was involved in another one of Walter's dream gifts. No one knows about it but Edmond and the two of us. I was the deliverer of the precious gift to the lady in another church. I told her just "Praise the Lord" for answered prayer. While there, I prayed for another lady and her husband who both had cancer at the time, and as of this date (October 7, 2008), they are both still healed. Thank God. When I returned to let Walter know how it all went, he wanted no credit, just give God the glory. I said to him that I can't wait to see how the Lord will bless us all. Just last week, I thought on this and it came to me. This trip to Israel is my blessing. I've been so happy and grateful and so looking forward to the trip now. My head has been there for a while, but now my heart is also.

I have had so much fun packing and unpacking my suitcases and putting on my clothes. My daughter Leah has sent several outfits. I will be attending the Feast of Tabernacles, which occurs on the seventh month of the year and lasts seven days. Just to think, I was married for fifty-seven years; my husband went home to be with the Lord on the twenty-seventh of the year 2007 at age seventy-seven. So many sevens. I even gave birth to seven daughters. The number seven is special to me in light of what it means biblically, which means complete. Someday I'll write about my life without him but that will be another time.

Our journey will begin on October 11 at around 1:00 a.m., as Sister Annie and I will be on our way to catch our plane in Indianapolis. Oh yes, getting your bills paid, calling people, writing notes (my goodness), checking your health insurance plan to see if it worked overseas. Guess what? It didn't work outside of the United States. What a bummer! It wasn't easy getting all your ducks in a row. Edmond would say, "Keep trying, you can do it." And I did by the grace of God.

You know, when you decide to take a trip and especially an awesome trip like this, the people who love you also want to have a part. They like to call and come and say good-bye by bringing something. One example is our good friend and brother who came with a monetary gift. I said to him, "Do you think I'm going to leave all my money in Israel?"

"No," he said, "but maybe you will see something you can't do without."

Oh yeah, me, a seventy-four-year-old can't do without. Ha-ha!

Well, I got my carry-on bag packed and took it over to my traveling buddy who had my plane ticket. She was going to weigh it. We talked and laughed for a bit and then put my suitcase on the scale. Guess what? My bag was overweight, so I had to take my peanut M&M's out. Now these are my favorite snacks, so I'll have to come up with something else to take out.

Meanwhile, my pastor Jay and his wife, Jana, came for a visit, and we talked about the trip. We discussed all the miracles the Lord had worked in my life toward this trip. I also left some advice for them toward shepherding the flock for Jesus. They were taking over leadership of the church since Edmond's passing. Edmond and I had shared many things with the both of them. For example, it takes a great love of God and wisdom to follow through. I know my husband did it for twenty-nine years. Thank God! He left a foundation for them to build upon. I just shared with them to love the Lord and feed the sheep as Jesus had instructed Peter.

Day before Departure
October 9, 2008

This is the last day before my departure. I am up early having heard the chimes on my clock at 6:00 a.m. I rolled over and got up; it is yet dark outside. This last week, I told myself I was going to rest. Ha! Rest? What is that? There is always something to think of and do. Today I will start with, "Oh, Lord, giving you thanks for waking me and letting me be in my right mind and health to accomplish the things needed to be done for me." I rearranged my overloaded suitcase and packed the large one. I love the early morning; it is so quiet, calm, and peaceful. I hear the clock ticking, and my mind is just thinking faster than I can write. I am sitting on the side of my bed having just put drops in my eyes and thanking the Lord that that is my only health problem.

I've finished reading the first five books of the Bible; 187 chapters in all. I wanted to read them before leaving for Israel—the Holy Land. As Isaiah said, speaking about the beautiful city—the Holy City of Jerusalem;

"How beautiful upon the mountains are the feet of him that bringeth good tidings that publisheth peace; that bringeth good tidings of good, that publisheth salvation; that saith unto Zion—thy God reigneth!" (Isaiah 52:7, KJV).

The day is breaking and Janice (our longtime family friend and Edmonds' farming buddy) has gone by on the school bus. I hear my only son, Eddie—more commonly known as Uncle Bub in the family—and his wife, Kristi, stirring and getting ready for work. I'm still sitting on the side of the bed. My second order of the day is to finish and send some thank you notes and then I will go from there.

This is the eve just before leaving tomorrow night. I finished my notes, answered many calls, and went to get my nails manicured. It wasn't very pleasant as the lady wasn't very good, but I smiled and said to myself, "Well, I helped her." I then went to get pampered by getting my hair washed, but the lady that normally shampoos my hair wasn't there. This didn't go too well either, but I'm being a help to others today. I came home for a bite of lunch and then took a nap. Afterwards, the phone rang and I'm up again. God is so good. A church member stopped by and had a not-so-good news health-wise. I was blessed to be able to pray for him. Oh Lord, grant him peace.

On my last morning before takeoff, the Lord woke me. I rolled over and went to the little girl's room and brushed my teeth. So I'll just lay back down and rest. My, my, that didn't happen because the light in my mind turned on. I began to think that maybe I should take two packages of dried prunes to keep the system working, can't have any clogging in the old country (my body!). My mind shifted to my oldest friend, Lunolia, who is having eye surgery this morning. I began to pray for her. We go way back to the days when we attended Patoka Church and Sunday school together. We had enough children between us to have a couple of classes or more. She had eleven; and me, with a small group of six. Wow!

It's now 6:55 a.m. and the big yellow school bus with the number 23 just went by—saw it through the window. So the lights are on and with pen in hand, I decided to put to paper a few things. The day is beginning to dawn, it's just a little cool and the heavy dew on the ground looks like shining diamonds on the grass. Today will be my last time to sleep in my bed for two weeks. That will be different. But you know what? Jesus didn't have a place to lay His royal head. I'm going to see and remember well some of the things He went through just for me. When things are not as comfortable for me on the trip, I will remember my blessed Savior.

I have got to get my money into all my secret hiding places. Hope I can find it when I need it. Maybe I should make a map. Hmm…probably not a good idea if I lose the paper. The sun is up and shining through the trees and onto the grass, making a beautiful glitter. The trees are beginning to turn. My, what a beautiful sight when I return in two weeks. The browns, oranges, and yellow gold. Oh yes! Did I forget to tell you that I live on a farm with trees all around the edge of the pasture. When you sit outside you can see the beautiful black and red cattle with white faces, eating and lying down next to the pond. What a lovely sight!

By the way, Ruth Ann and Ken and my grandsons are flying across the world right now (well, almost) as they are going from coast to coast to be able to meet me and my traveling buddy in New York. Isn't that wonderful? They are leaving while I'm writing this passage at 9:30 a.m. on Friday—6:30 a.m., California time. My word—God bless them with safety.

Oh yes, I must tell you about when I was packing. I tried on all my clothes and had a style show for my daughters—Tina (one of my twins), Pam (my second daughter and third child who lives just down the road from me), and my daughter in love, Kristi. They all took pictures and sent them around the family in Indianapolis and California with their phones. Here we go again with the twenty-first century and its gadgets! What will be next, you say? Well, just read on.

I just received a call from my gift giver, Walter, with such a wonderful testimony since he helped me. He had asked the Lord a favor to allow him to get out of debt. You guessed it. On the same eve that I'm flying out, he is now paying off credit cards and other bills. Isn't God the best! The more you give, the more He gives back. We serve an awesome God. I'm praying and asking the Lord to bless everyone who has been so helpful in making this trip possible.

One such testimony of blessing was when the young girl whose mother and sister we had helped over thirty years ago was blessed with a good business, being in the precise place at the right time, and having been sent to the right person to talk to at the exact time. It all went well for her. Children, don't forget, the Lord gives to us so that we can give to others.

I've had a small nap now and waiting for the children to return from shopping. They came back with the wrong disc for the camera and it's five hours before leaving home. Oh well, Lord, I believe and trust your care. Thank You.

Its 11:30 p.m. I am up getting myself together and listening to the gospel music. God is good. The day is breaking outside and our dog, Patches, realizes that something is going on in the house. The lights are burning and there are more movements than other nights. The stars are shining, and I am waiting for my traveling buddy. Annie's other son, Scott, and wife, Julie, will be bringing her to my house. Eddie and Kristi were resting. They'd had a very long day and will be driving us to Indianapolis. Today was Kristi's fortieth birthday. Hope she knows that life begins at forty—oh yea! I'm too excited for sleeping. I tried to take a nap but the telephone woke me. My mind is working overtime, making sure and very sure that all is well here, and that I have all I need to go. Ruth Ann and

Ken have arrived safely in New York at their appointed time. Thank God.

My friend of four years, Dessie, who is eighty-four, called to have a prayer with me and said, "Remember the angels of mercy and grace shall follow you." There is a wonderful friendship between us. We met just before her eightieth birthday. We had never heard nor ever seen one another. When she was told about me, she had no desire to fellowship because of who she thought I was. When we met, we bonded, and ever since became very great friends. Another blessing of the Lord who put us together.

Before leaving, I wanted to know why Walter wanted to send me and how it came about, because I wanted to give my testimony once I arrived in Israel. I could say, "It's because of another person's dream." He was laying down saying to the Lord that he wanted to go to the Holy Land when the Lord told him to send Sister Frances. Wow! When he woke up, he began to process the dream and think about what the Lord meant. He knew he was to obey the Lord in this." So when I am asked about how I got to Israel, I'll be ready. My head got there long before my heart.

I've done so much packing and unpacking that the thought came to me, *You will wear out the clothes before ever wearing them.* But as the old saying goes, "If there isn't another day, you won't need it."

I had another thought about the card I received from the young lady who we helped over thirty years ago. I was standing in the back door of my home just looking out at the cows grazing in the pasture. The phone rang, and my friend Walter asked, "Are you ready and do you feel good about going?"

"My head is there, but my heart is just not there yet." As I said this, it was like a bolt of lightning that hit me. The Lord said the trip was my blessing from asking Him after we had done a great thing for someone else. I had remarked at the time, "I sure wonder what God has in store for us after this." The Lord reminded me of this and said, "Your blessing is your trip to the Holy Land." My heart got with my head and excited about two weeks before leaving. I have no fear, just joy.

THE JOURNEY BEGINS
OCTOBER 10, 2008

We arrived at the airport in Indy very early in the morning. It is still dark outside, and the airport is not yet ready for business. My son and wife dropped us off and said good-bye. They will be spending the weekend in Indy. My traveling partner, Ms. Annie, and I go inside, and because it is so early, some people are sleeping on the benches. We get our tickets out and Ms. Annie asks me, "Do you have your…"

"Yes, I have my passport," I replied.

Annie gets excited and says, "Oh, you need your driver's license."

"I don't think so, Annie."

Annie's mind began to work. My son has already left the airport and there is nothing open. Annie decided to call Ken in New York and ask. Ken and Ruth Ann didn't answer (they must still be asleep). Annie leaves a message. Ken calls back and tells her we only need our passports. Our minds are at ease. I'm hoping Ken can go back to sleep. We won't leave until 7:00 a.m. and scheduled to arrive at 9:20 a.m. in New York.

The airport is beginning to get busy. We check our luggage at the curb and stopped and get some coffee and hot chocolate. "Hot" chocolate is just like its name—too hot and takes so long to drink. I finally finish it and—oh my, just a few hours ago, the airport was empty, and now, the line is getting long. People are coming out of the woodwork. Now the trip is getting real. We go through security line and Ms. Annie can't find her ticket and boarding pass. The security man wanted to send us back, but thank God she finds it. Our flight to New York is good and Ken was there to meet us when we arrived. That was grand. Our trip had begun.

A SHORT STAY IN NEW YORK
OCTOBER 10, 2008

I've never been to New York before. All the things I've read about and seen on TV, I will now be able to see. What a treat. Ken picked us up in the hotel bus which took us back to where they were staying. They had breakfast, but we didn't get anything to eat on the plane, except for orange juice. When we got back to where Ken and Ruth Ann were staying, it looked like China town. The hotel was nice and seeing the grandchildren was great. All seven of us were together now and would be traveling together for the rest of the trip. What a blessing! Two grandmothers with their children and grandchildren.

After breakfast and checkout, we loaded up our luggage into a limousine that was taking us around New York for a few hours. Wow! A long black sleek limo. Nothing else, except a bus or truck, would have been able to hold our luggage. This was so much fun. Our driver told us his name was Sonny. Ken said, "That must be your nickname, what's your real name?"

"Shlomo," he says.

"Where are you originally from?" Ken asked.

"Israel," Sonny says. We were all so blessed to hear that God had given us a driver from our destination. He was very nice and pleasant and took us all around the city. We got to see the Statue of Liberty, Museum of Jewish Heritage, New Jersey across the water, Greenwich Village, the American Express Building, and Ground Zero. Oh Lord, my heart was pounding and wept for the lost ones and the living who remained; all of them were in my prayers this day. America is the home of many people—brothers, sisters, and family. We all have experienced the pain of losing someone, so we know the pain that our brothers and sisters have endured here and to also where we are going (Israel). Only God can heal a broken heart, and we must give him all the pieces. Moving on—not much time to cry.

We also saw the West Side of Manhattan; Shea Stadium, home of the NY Mets; and Canal Street going into SOHO, home of famous designer apartments ($500,000 bedrooms). My Lord, I am so grateful for the farm back in Indiana. It's not grand, but it is our home. We also went to Sixth Avenue, which was officially called Avenue of the Americas.

The driver told us that 11–12 million people are in and out of Manhattan every day. Wow!

Macy's 150 years old. Now when I see the commercials about New York City on TV, I'll be thinking, I saw that. Little old me at the Diamond District in 47th Street.

Speaking of diamonds, this takes me back to Christmas 2007, two days before Jesus came and got my husband of fifty-seven years. Edmond, while in his hospital bed, gave me a ring that day before going home to be with the Lord. To me, that ring was the crown jewel. It could not have been any more precious.

Times Square: The next New Year's when the ball is dropped, I can say I was there. Interesting isn't it? At seventy-four years old. My, my.

Brooklyn Bridge: We took a family picture at the pier looking back toward Manhattan. Now it's time to go to JFK airport to catch our flight to Israel.

ALL FIRST TIME AT SEVENTY-FOUR YEARS YOUNG

OCTOBER 10, 2008

While waiting in line to check our luggage at JFK, more of our friends arrive from California. It was wonderful to see them (Paul, Mary, Rikki, and Olivia). We had seen them just last year in California while visiting. It is a beautiful thing to watch people in large places (small ones also), but so much goes on in large places. There was a small African family all dressed up in their blues and purples which was very stylish. Their children were running and playing. I wondered why they had so much duct tape on their luggage and packages. Well, I sure found out after mine arrived at our destination. The duct tape kept the luggage from ripping at the seams from all the rough handling. That African family sure knew how to travel. Remember, you're never too old to learn.

We boarded an international Swiss airplane. My, what a large airplane. I looked out the window and the wing just kept going and going. There were eight seats across each row—two on each side and four in the middle. There were four toilets, two on each aisle.

The Swiss flight was like a big family. There were people of all races, but everyone was nice. The attendants were so kind, and you sure wouldn't go hungry because they feed you well. The meals were warm and the snacks were great too. The ride to Zurich was good. When we arrived, there wasn't much time before our next flight. It would have been great to see the city, but we only had time to shop and visit the ladies' room. Now we're on our way to Tel Aviv.

I was able to rest some on the flight. The clouds looked like puffs of cotton. When we landed, the lights sparkled like diamonds and Christmas lights. We arrived, went through customs and check points, and all went well. Our guide met us outside of the Tel Aviv airport in a lovely tour bus with a nice driver. We rode for about two and a half hours through the countryside to the Dead Sea. Along the way, the land was just rocks, sand, and dirt. We saw such high mountains and the road was good, but very narrow and curvy. The people in the other cars just passed us by, and I'm thinking, *My goodness, look at that*, but they must know where they're going and how to get there—at least I hope so. We saw small houses off in the distance and larger ones as well. We also saw green areas which indicated there must be water close by. Where there was water, they must have had to dig down to find it, then run some pipe and irrigate. There must have been a spring underground. We saw a couple of boys leading a donkey and all at once they began hitting him. This reminded me of the prophet who was saved by an ass (who talked) and kept his master from an angel with a sword. I thought maybe something was in the way that was keeping the donkey from moving.

The guide would tell us that anytime we saw a patch or grove of trees, there would of course be water around. It looked very strange to drive for miles and miles and see nothing but brown and sand, and then come upon a green orchard of trees. Look at God.

After riding for miles, we saw some large homes and finally arrived at the Crowne Plaza Hotel resting between large tall beautiful mountains surrounded by the Dead Sea. The hotel was nice. I just wanted to walk in the sea, so I put on my jelly shoes, pulled up my skirt, took the hand of my grandson, and walked out into the water. Oh my! The feeling was like being in a large amount of lotion. If you walked too far, you would float, which some of the people were doing.

They said there was healing in the sea because of all the minerals in the water. You could see the white salt around the edge. I was so blessed to be there, praying and thinking that I had read about this and now I'm here. The night was dark, beautiful, and so peaceful. We ate a wonderful meal—the buffet had many choices including salads, soup, and breads. After the meal, we went to bed. I noticed that the salt on the tail of my skirt had caused it to be so stiff that the skirt could stand alone.

I awoke early the next morning and looked out the window at the people in the sea. But the most wonderful thing about the morning was watching the sun come up over the sea and watching it continue to rise higher and higher. The sun was shining like a diamond from the sky. While watching this and praying, the Lord gave me the following revelation: "I scattered my chosen and I'll bring them back home." Oh my! I was so excited. I told Annie and witnessed to others that were along with us. One thing about it is that God sees and hears our cry and will come to our rescue right on time. There is an old saying, "He may not come when we want but He's always on time." That day started wonderfully, and I took pictures of those beautiful graceful mountains which surrounded the sea and hotel.

We are back on the bus going to where the Dead Sea Scrolls were written. Once we arrived, we saw a movie about the men who wrote the scrolls. It was very interesting. We learned before writing any word or sentence down they would repeat it over and over to make sure they did not make any mistakes. Also, these men did not allow any gossiping or talking about other things because they were so dedicated to their writing.

We returned to the bus after such a wonderful experience. I was thinking that is how our life for Christ should be lived every day. Doing unto others the way we want others to return the deed. Oh yes! When reading the word, I find if we read it out loud, it sinks in better because you have less time for thinking of other stuff while reading. I will never be able to put to paper all the awesome feelings you get just being in the places of Kings, Prophets, and Jesus and His disciples. My Lord, what a blessing!

2,000 year old Olive Tree

Ancient Galilee Boat

Aronson Home in Jerusalem

Baptism in Jordan River

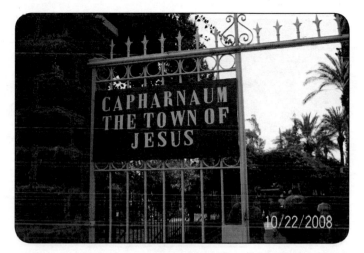

Capharnaum

Cloud in Jerusalem

Eating in the Sukkot in Jerusalem

Family at the Mediterranean

Friends from Africa

Friends on the boat to Galilee

Illegal Immigration Camp

Illegal Immigration Camp

Jerusalem

Ken, Ruth, and Kuri Wallis, @ site of the
finding of the Dead Sea Scrolls

Mediterranean Sea

Annie and I in NYC

A friend from Indiana I ran into at the march in Jerusalem

Me in NYC

Night at the Dead Sea

Pastor Paul and Mary @ the Feast

Sunrise over the Dead Sea

Yad Vashem Memorial

Outside the Aronson Home in Jerusalem

Me reading my book to my dear friend Miss Frances

MASADA

OCTOBER 13, 2008

Annie and I woke up early, went downstairs to eat breakfast, and then planned the day. We had a choice of either going to the spa or taking a cable car ride to Masada. I had decided to take the cable car ride before I had ever left Indiana. This was such an interesting tour. I really didn't think it would be so high and such a large cable car. I was thinking it would be more like a ski lift. Boy, was I surprised that the car held about thirty or forty people. It was really full. Being so close to a few friends and many strangers very high up in the air made for a very humbling experience. There was also a walking path, but you would have to be in good health to take that path up to the top. It would have taken me a couple of days.

After the ride, we got off the cable car and had to walk up some stairs and over the area of ground seeing how Herod's fortress was built. We saw many rooms, one of which was his bathroom. It was amazing how the water was directed from the mountain all the way down and piped to his bath. Herod built a lot of rooms and a very large palace.

We were told that over nine hundred Jewish people took their lives instead of surrendering to the Romans in AD 73. It made me think what an awful thing to do, especially if there is no other way out. Sometimes we forget where the Lord has brought us from and who is on our side. As you read this, I want to say that the Lord has been all things to my husband and me. We praise him in all things. When the flood comes, remember that He has the boat along with the paddles or the motor, one would say.

On the way down from the mountain, we had to hurry and catch the cable car. There were so many getting on. We were packed in, and one of the girls was claustrophobic and had to get off. She began to sweat. I began to pray, and she ended up catching the next cable car.

We waited at the gift shop at the base of the mountain. Oh yes, our cable car was driven by automation and not by a pulley on the way down the mountain to the dessert.

In the evening, we were attending the first night of the feast celebration outside. The gates opened at 5:00 p.m. There were four to five people deep in line for what seemed like miles. There were many busses unloading more and more people. It was a first come, first served situation. Those that got their first would get a seat, and others would have to sit on the ground. When God took the children of Israel out of Egypt, they were over six hundred thousand and had to sit on the ground. And just think, God fed them from heaven with the heavenly manna.

We were very blessed. There were seven thousand there to be fed the evening meal. I was so fascinated by the crowd. I truly can't remember what I ate, but just to think, Moses had twelve tribes to take care of and tonight, we had people from over one hundred countries. Words can't describe the sight or the feeling. The lines went very fast, and I didn't hear any complaining or murmuring about the wait or the long lines.

Ms. Annie left to go to the bathroom. We waited and kept moving in the line, watching the many beautiful people. Time went on and no Ms. Annie. Kuri went to look and couldn't find her. Ruth and Ken then went searching for her, and finally told Pastor Paul we couldn't find her. You know what? I was never afraid. As we got closer to the gate, guess what? You guessed it—Annie was there. She thought we would be closer to the gate so she went there and waited. We could not understand or speak the language of many people there, but our smiles and the love of God spoke for us.

When we entered the gate with all the people, I realized I was a part of the Micah prophecy in chapter 4. We were at the mountain close to the Dead Sea with people from many nations praising God, speaking of Jacob and the Lion of the Tribe of Judah. There was peace and no mention of war. There was a spirit of hope and joy. I can't explain in words how I truly felt in that place.

MARCH DAY
OCTOBER 16, 2008

I woke up early and began to think of the many people in Jerusalem on the march. While walking and looking at the faces, we saw a girl on the porch of a high building that looked so much like my Susie in California. It caused me to think that we are all shapes and colors in the same overall race of God. Brown, lighter, darker—it doesn't matter. We are all the same. Just remember at the tower of Babel that God didn't change people's color, just their language. I saw people that looked just like me until they opened their mouth. There was no difference. So until we all speak the same language, we can communicate with love, caring, and respect. The Jews are God's chosen, but we are adopted and grafted in to His family. Oh, praise the Lord. Speaking of family, I said to Crystal and Susie, "Wouldn't it be awesome if I met someone who knew me?" That's exactly what happened. A lady from a small town in Monroe City, Indiana, came up to me and said, "I know you. I've met you before." She had been to my church in Indiana. I thought, *Wow, amazing.* For just that part of the march, the people lined the street, crying out in their Hebrew language. Those who spoke English would say, "Welcome, America" or "Thank you, America, for coming." It was very touching. There were such beautiful faces, but some looked tired and worried also. I've never felt such a strong and wonderful feeling inside of me as I walked, gave away candy and American flags, waved, and asked God's blessing on the crowd. And it was quite a crowd. There were people on the rooftops and on the street side. We had to be careful not to get separated from the rest of our US group. But I was never afraid. Ken and Larry (the pastor leader of our tour group) were the last in the US group carrying the American flag. I'm so glad to be an American. Despite all the problems we have in America, I would not want to live anywhere else.

I don't know how far we walked, but it was a very long way up the grade. I was looking at all the people, taking pictures of the beautiful families in their attire and trying to keep up!

What I gathered from the people was that they were one as a family. I saw fathers, mothers, and children together. We couldn't always speak their language, but a smile of love in our heart is always understood. I was so very tired, but in the midst of my tiredness, a face would appear or a voice heard, and I would get a new stride in my step. It was awesome. Jesus said that perfect love casts out all fear. I witnessed that in the march and in the country.

I could have easily gotten lost in the crowd and never surfaced again—it was that many people. There were people in the march dressed in their native clothes. I would have loved to see the march, but you can't march and watch at the same time! This is something everyone should do once. If I ever go back, I will take all that I can to give away during the march (we were giving candy to the children). I had a little to give away and wished I had more, but nothing kept me from praying for them and us during the march. Even though the walk was long, it was over before we knew it. God Bless His Chosen and Us.

THE HILL AT GOLGOTHA
AND THE TOMB
OCTOBER 18, 2008

We left the hotel on the bus with our faithful guide and wonderful careful bus driver. We made several other stops before arriving, and we were on a timetable because many people were here to take communion. When our time arrived, we were at the hill and were met by another guide who told us the history of the tomb of Jesus and about Golgotha Hill. It was beautiful there as the flowers were still in bloom. We walked up to where we could see the skull embedded in the stone. Of course, my mind went back to the word I had read. Can you imagine how the spirit of love came over me while remembering Jesus was nailed to the cross just for me, and now two thousand years later, I am here! I felt the spirit all over me knowing it is the presence of the Lord Jesus. After the remembrance of His Last Supper, we walked to the tomb and went inside. What an awesome feeling. Someday, I will see His face in peace and hearing the words, "Well done." He was there in the tomb and now is not as He is at the right hand of His Father. God will return for us—His bride. We also took communion there. I thought about what Jesus said, "As often as you eat my body and drink my blood," I will remember Him until He returns.

BETHLEHEM
OCTOBER 14, 2008

We walked to the site of seeing where Jesus was born but could not go over as the area does not allow Jewish people to come in (our guide and driver were Jewish). The place was so serene and beautiful with an arch that was covered with flowers standing on the top of the hill. You could stand and look toward Bethlehem.

I began to think, *Where was my Savior born?* There are less and less of His people there as other races have taken much of the space. As I stood, the tears came, and sadness surrounded me all the while many of the others touring with us were taking pictures underneath the arch, laughing and talking about other things. My mind remembered the Word—a baby was born in a lowly place with just his mother and father, but God was looking on and had a plan for that beautiful baby. The shepherds would leave all and come to see Him. I'm thinking, children, we must leave all to come to Him and let His Spirit rest in our lowly hearts—where there used to be no room. This is my prayer for the people of Israel now.

Then came the angelic choir from heaven singing "Glory to the Highest." I thought that we aren't angels, but we can sing "Glory to the Highest" who lives in us. I'm so glad I opened the door to this not so nice stable and let the Savior in.

Then the wise men came with the wonderful gifts they brought. I thought about what I can give this King of kings. I would not give him gold because He has cattle on a thousand hills. But because I know He is the King of kings and royalty, I give Him my body, which is a living representative of His.

I looked toward Bethlehem for a good little while. Ruth said, "Come on, Mother," as the group had begun to leave. I wanted to take a picture. I took one just overlooking the city. It's amazing how far you can see if you have good eyes which I don't have now at seventy-four, but I'm so thankful that I can see and the eyesight of my heart is great. Oh yes, I almost forgot. As the other people have taken over the city, we must not let the enemy take over what the town of Bethlehem means to us.

We walked back to the bus. I'm sure I missed so many of the beautiful sites on the way back as my mind was still at the birth and growing up of Jesus and what is happening there now. But you know, the wonderful thing about it all is Jesus the Son and God the Father knows and sees it all and hears our prayers and sees our tears. I know He will restore His chosen people at His appointed time.

Children, the other thing about Bethlehem before Christ was that many other historical sites and events happened there. The death and burial of Rachel, whom Jacob loved and worked so hard for before becoming Israel—the head of God's chosen. David anointed king by Samuel and also the great story of Ruth and Boaz.

This was the awesome thing about Israel. No matter where we went, history just kept coming. It's no wander people continue going back over and over again. I understand that more and more after being there. God told Moses to remind the people over and over how He had brought them out of Egypt with a strong arm. We must continue telling our children about salvation and the love of Jesus, who is the first and last, Alpha and Omega; and Aleph and Tau, who also died for our sins. And, children, I'm telling you, we have and must continue living this wonderful, blessed, suffering life until Jesus returns.

Yad Vashem Memorial
October 15, 2008

The Lord woke me up with a message about a cloud. Not just any puff or cotton, but what led the children of Israel in the day. I was in Israel at the Yad Vashem Memorial walking through while the guide was telling us all about the things that had happened. Then the cries of the babies, young ones, and the old ones begin to dwell in my spirit, "How long, oh Lord, how long?"

In one particular place, it was dark, and the lights like faces would shine. My heart ached just to know the innocent that suffered at the hand of the devil, in the form of a man with a very black heart. So as I walked out, with many friends with us, I just stopped and began to pray in my heart. And then

I looked over the valley, the Lord showed me a cloud had appeared. One such as I had never seen, and I'm seventy-three years young. God is so awesome to show such beauty at the time of sorrow and who will someday wipe away all our tears. I took out my camera and took the grandest photo. It was as if the Lord was saying, "I led them by day and I've never left them. I hear their cries and see your sorrow and pain."

Two years after returning home, we were outside my house. It was really cold out. Soon, there appeared another cloud of remembrance which showed up in the sky. This one was like a pillar of fire, which led the children of Israel at night, giving them the light. It was not dark here, but late in the evening in Indiana, I was standing on my back stoop. A cloud appeared, all aglow with red small places of dark and white surrounding it. Oh God, my! It was the Father, Son, and the Holy Ghost continuing to guide us. My son saw it, and we all took pictures, not knowing the meaning at the time. Today, you, oh Lord, have woke me up to let me know that you have seen our tears and have heard our prayers. This was a sign that you are still watching over us, taking care of us, and will never leave us. Thank you, Lord, for revelation and faith. I believe with all of me.

DAILY REFLECTION
DECEMBER 5, 2008

Children, I was thinking of my trip as well when the thought came. All the many places I went, I never saw a picture of Jesus on walls or doors or anywhere. Something else I didn't think of was Him in my mind like we see him here today. It's snowing on the door, and I'm in Crystal's bedroom watching Granddad rest, and guess what? I looked up and there I saw the picture, holding a lamb. Well, no wonder Isaiah said, "He has no form or comeliness and when we see Him, there is no beauty that we should desire Him." It's Jesus spirit, the spirit of love that touches and draws our hearts. That's what I felt in the garden when remembering on

His word. Why He was there and why He came just for me. It brought tears to my eyes and a very warm glow to my heart.

In walking or riding in a cab or on the city bus, something else occurred to me: *Where are the small wooden houses?* Wow! I didn't see any even after we left Jerusalem. The stone apartment and home connected together. Our tour bus then went to the famous garden. You must have an appointment before visiting there. It's large but not that large. While sitting on our tour bus, waiting, I noticed some children playing on what we would call a sidewalk, but it was really a yard of concrete. Cars parked on the street, a gate and fence around it. The little boys kept teasing a man to open his car door, because of a puppy in the window. Every time the man would come and set off his alarm, they ran. So I'm wondering, *Where are the parents of these small children so close to the street?* After a while of teasing, the children finally ran out of sight, I suppose to play somewhere else.

One other thing while looking at the children playing reminded me of my childhood. As I have said earlier, we moved around a lot. This time I'm in Tennessee at my uncle Jeff's house. They had a very high porch where I could play under in the dirt, and I did a lot of that by myself. At times I was a doctor healing everything no matter what it was, if it looked hurt or sick. Other times I was a mother, wanted five children, and I was never going to move; just stay with my husband and raise my children. I would always tell myself that just when I would be making my mud pies, my aunt

Carrie would call me to feed the pigs. I remember carrying some weeds to them called horseweeds. It sounded strange feeding horseweeds to hogs. We were taken to church by our grandmother Joyner, who was no-nonsense inside the church. We had no children's church either. I can remember at a very early age when the preacher would talk about fire and hell and how the worms will crawl on you and they won't die. I never wanted to go to church, but hearing that made a believer out of me. So I knew I must be good, not only to go to heaven, but to be able to stay with my cousins in their home—the ones I stayed with the most and the longest were with Georgia and Margaret Ann and her brother whom we call Big Junior. They thought I was the best child. Whatever I was asked to do, I did it, not because I was so good but so they would let me stay. Little did I know the Lord had his hand on me the entire time?

In other places we went, they have houses that were so large and made of stone, they were so beautiful. One other thing, children, so many homes were left unfinished, it reminded me of Jesus saying, "Count the cost to see if you have sufficient funds" (Luke 14:28, KJV). Our guide said things happened out of their control. Speaking of counting the cost for a house, my husband, Edmond, was in the hospital having surgery and I went to see him the next day. He said to me, "I'm going to build you a new home." I just smiled. He said it again, and I said, "The medicine must be working with his head." A few days later, he came home, and I'm sure he was counting the cost. He went to his friends at the bank, but they turned him down, saying, "Edmond and Frances and all their kids can't pay." We weren't bitter about it, the Lord had a plan. Edmond was on the tractor working in the field, and he always sang or preached when the Lord spoke to his spirit. The Lord told him where to go and the man to ask for at another bank. He did it and all went well. We had a new house, and the Lord gave us favor in work, and we paid for it. When we built the house, Edmond had lost his job. It made it difficult for us to pay for the construction. Another man came along needing help and he ended up helping us instead. We stayed with him until the house was paid for, then the Lord took him home. The favor didn't stop, people needed help, and we were there. You can't beat God giving or supplying your needs, just trust him.

Children, just a few Sundays ago, I was teaching the Sunday school lesson, which I love to do—studying God's word. The subject was "the Lord Reigns" in the book of Micah 4:1–4. Micah, a minor prophet, but to me a great one had a vision and a God-given ability to see the future and to tell the people about it. As I was teaching, the wonderful thought came to me. With such passion during my visit to Israel, I'm a part of Micah's vision of so many years ago. At the feast in En Gedi, Micah said, "In the last days the mountain of the house of the Lord shall be established in the mountains and exalted above the hills and people shall flow into." When I was there, many nations were there with their flags, worshipping the Lord together. The wonderful feeling I got just thinking about it was a feeling of joy, peace, and love. Our God is going to take care of the strong nations who fight against us. So that someday soon we will beat our swords into plowshares and our spears into pruning hooks. We will not lift any harm toward each other just like the example at En Gedi. We will not be afraid anymore because the mouth of the Lord had spoken.

THE RIVER JORDAN
JANUARY 19, 2012

The Lord woke me up this morning early again; it was dark outside and reminded me of Jordan. We were there while the baptizing was going on, and my mind just played back how it would have felt seeing John the Baptist and also hearing "Behold, the Lamb of God" coming to be baptized of him. When a feeling of warmth inside works its way out, what joy it was hearing a woman speaking a different language wanting to be baptized with our group. Pastor Larry incited her to come right on in the water. It was awesome. It reminded me of an experience I had a long time ago with my husband. I was on the way to church with Linda, Eddie, Pam, and Priscilla while he was on his way to town to have fun with friends. Children never understand the power of prayer. My husband said when he topped the hill where the church stood at the bottom, the car just turned and stopped at the church. Now it was up to him. So he got out and went in. When the altar call was given, he gave his life to Jesus. He was being baptized in the Patoka River, and I wanted to be baptized also, even though I had been years earlier. So I walked to the river down the bank, then we really became one. Singing "Wade in the Water." Guess what part of that song says "'Who's that coming all dressed in white, must be the children of the Israelites. At the Jordan they were dressed in white-my my to be there at that time was such a blessing. So many groups there and many people on the bank just made you wonder what we came to see.'"

THE FEAST OF THE TABERNACLE

OCTOBER 13, 2008

I know I spoke of this earlier in my writings. It began at En Gedi; afterwards we went to Jerusalem. Riding the bus there as we sang, my eyes filled with tears just thinking of Jesus's last stop trip here to give his life for me. We rode around the town seeing it at night; it was beautiful. Our hotel which was very nice was within walking distance to the feast. We would take the tours on the bus then rush back to get ready for the feast, just like heaven to me. I have never seen or been with so many people praising God. We stood in a long line just waiting to get into the convention center.

Fellowshipping with the people in line was awesome. Some had traveled from faraway places like us from the USA, and others from Germany, Denmark, Africa, Finland, and Ireland, just to name a few. One of the most fantastic things to me was all the volunteers who paid their own way and used their vacation time just to work at the feast. What a blessing! It reminded me of when I first came to know the Lord Jesus as the pardon of my sins. I was so happy to work in the church doing whatever my hands found me to do, and I did it. Dad and I organized a bus ministry, only it was a car, and we didn't know it was called a ministry. We just realized that people needed a ride to church. I was a very active member in the church body. I did everything such as being a janitor, being superintendent of Sunday school, being a teacher—you name it, I did it. We even made fires on a pot belly stove before service to keep us warm. We were happy as could be to serve the body of Christ. The crowd would gather in the music and praise dances, and we would join in the Spirit of the Lord, which fell in that place. I have never seen a full orchestra before with members from many countries. It was a little bit of heaven. When the conductor stepped on what I called "that little box" and tapped, the music began. My, my, you just felt like flying away to be at rest. After the praise, then the word. Each night was just wonderful, all speaking toward the subject title: "The Lion of Judah." Each guest speaker gave us a new thought and carried us a little higher each night. My remembrances of Jesus and the twelve disciples having communion together, this was such a spirit-filled awesome glorious time. You looked over the crowd all in white like angels everywhere and taking the Lord's supper together. There are no words for me to describe this wonderful time. We may not have been in the upper room, but I was in the balcony, and in Jerusalem. My Lord, what a blessing! My heart was so full; I took the celebration of the supper back to share with my church family in Indiana.

When I arrived home that Christmas eve in 2008, I got permission from my pastor to have the Lord's Supper. I brought the message and paid tribute to my husband, Edmond. Then we all dressed in white with candlelight. We read the Bible in multiple languages, English, Spanish, and Chinese, all while holding a candle. We deeply reflected on what Jesus had done for us on the cross. Remembering His death and His resurrection. Oh, Lord, may we never turn our backs to the wall...Jesus. Also, during the feast, we were entertained by special musical guests from China. The Chinese Christians from mainland China performed with twenty musicians who appeared in the opening celebration of the 2008 Olympics in Beijing. Just think, we saw them on TV and now in person. I also saw and heard the Israeli children's choir, whose voices touch the sky with harmonious singing, and the dancing was simply breathtaking. It was a phenomenal experience through it all. The written word coming from the guest speakers through the translators were incredible. When the praises went up, the blessings came down! The many countries marching and waving their flags was something to see. When we all get to heaven, what a day of rejoicing that will be. One of our friends from California, Pastor Paul, was part of the communion service. It made us feel as though we had a part in the feast too.

THE ILLEGAL
IMMIGRATION CAMP
OCTOBER 15, 2008

This was not on our tour, but the guide was so gracious in taking us to interesting places if we had time. This was something to see. Much of this started the year I was born in 1934. I've never been to prison, so this gave me a very uneasy feeling of how it must have felt to be behind barbed wire and watched by unkind people. There they sat on a bus to haul them like cattle into prison. When we first arrived, they told of the history. We walked around the grounds and went inside the barracks. It was such a small place to house so many people. We saw pictures of family and friends on the walls, just hoping and wondering if they would ever return. My heart took me back to the old stories told to us of the slaves coming to America and what awful conditions they were in. We also saw the great stone bath where they were forced to take off their clothes and were then placed into a disinfecting vat: women on one side and men on the other. No doors, no privacy of any kind. Such shame.

You know, children, I'm so glad that Jesus came in love and took our shame on the tree. We can love each other and remember how we want to be treated and do so likewise. My husband and I had such love for Israel because we believed the word told to Abraham. If he was blessed, we would be also, and those that worked against him would be cursed. This was quite an experience. It took me back to the age of my people, The American Indians, Africans, and Black Americans. I just pray that as we read the word of God, we realize that one blood made us all and that Jesus, a Jewish man, died so that we all may become one in Him. So, children, never forget to pray for our nation and all the people of the Lord.

I was just sitting here writing and thinking of some of the interesting things I did and places I saw. For instance, we rode in a jeep, saw people camping along the Jordan River, and we saw mango trees. At the top of the overlook, we took pictures in front of what they called "The Jesus Tree," a thorny tree whose branches they used to make the crown for His head.

We also saw what they called "holy raspberries," which was given their name because they have three leaves. We stopped where Jesus fed the five thousand and had twelve leftover baskets. On the bus going to another location, we passed by what the Jewish people called "the Shouting Wall." Friends and loved ones were separated by this wall and shouted messages back and forth because crossing to the other side was not allowed. We saw the Hermon Stream at Park Banias, and we passed the coast of Ceasarea-Philippi where Jesus asked his disciples, "Who do men say that I am?" Children, I am so glad I can answer that statement just as the disciples answered it long ago: Jesus, the Christ, and son of God.

The next day, we left early for the Sea of Galilee, where Jesus taught the Sermon on the Mount. While sitting there, we read the Beatitudes. There is a church built at that site now. We can only imagine how it must have been with so many people sitting on the ground and our Lord speaking beautiful words of, "Blessed are the peacemakers..." We truly need peacemakers here in Israel today. Ken picked up a rock for me to bring home from the Sea of Galilee at St. Peter's. Primacy—the place where Jesus asked, "Do you love me, more than these?" and then cooked fish for the disciples. We stopped and toured a home of a family named Aharonson, who had many struggles and tragedies in their lives. One of the more interesting stories for me was concerning one of the young men. He must have enjoyed eating dates as he kept the seeds in his pocket. When he died and was laid to rest in the ground, a seed that remained in his pocket began to grow, leaving a date tree behind as a remembrance of his death. *How lovely*, I thought to myself. What a wonderful way to be memorialized. I continued to pray that the life I love will speak for me.

WESTERN WALL
OCTOBER 16, 2008

We went to the Western Wall, some call the Wailing Wall. I'm sure many tears were shed here. It's a very fascinating place with many people standing around and many Jews with different headdresses on to say who they were. As we were walking, my thought was, "I've seen this many times on TV, now I'm standing here in the midst of it." The men prayed on one side of it, and the women altogether on the other side. I could hear them and see them writing on paper, and then finding a crack to place the request in. I did likewise. I am so grateful that at any time I can go to my prayer closet and talk with the Lord. One thing of interest when leaving the wall was that no one turned their back to the wall. We just backed out while others were coming in. This reminded me of where it says in the word about if you look back, you are not fit for the kingdom. We must keep our eyes on Jesus, where our help comes from. As I look back over my life, I can truly say that if it had not been for the Lord on my side, I would not be standing here and able to witness this great sight. Just being one of the many people coming here over the years.

Early this morning before daybreak as I was still lying in bed, my mind began to think on my tour of Israel, especially all the sites I saw and of the people of God. I thought of how I walked where they walked and the life they lived, the moving about from place to place. But mostly, I thought about all the love God had for them and myself, my husband, and our eight children that we raised. I too was somewhat like the Israelites. My mother moved a lot, though not for the same reasons of course. Then, like Jacob talking to his sons, I began to think on my family beginning with my eldest, Linda. She is kind, a helper to young people, and one who will share her home if you need a place to stay. My only son, Eddie, and his wife, Kristi, whose big heart is willing to help wherever and whomever he can, no matter what. Our Pam and Sam, what can I say! She is an example of Jesus: caring, calling, and sending cards to the sick. (At the time of writing this, she has a friend who is 101 years old and never complains. The Lord continues to bless her with health.) Priscilla and Edwin, they are so precious because of their love of God and how they care for the pastor and first lady. This is close to my heart because I once was a First Lady and the Lord sent me a helper. What a blessing they were. Our fifth child whom we call Susie, but her real name is Leah. She and her husband, Dale, are ministers of the word and servants of Christ. She loves the seniors, the children, and to praise and worship with the family of God. Ruth, my baby of eleven years, and her husband, Ken; she is a prayer warrior whose big heart aches to help young people by offering them Godly council and hospitality by opening her home to many. The end of my crop was multiplied; they came two at a time. The twins—Crystal and Christina—served on our church praise team, visited the sick in the hospitals and nursing homes, and sang for us at funerals, training for this day. Crystal and Adam help his parents, singing on the worship team at their church. She teaches children with disabilities. Christina is working at the church wherever she's needed. Like the Word says, "Whatever your hands find to do, do it."

I just thank God for giving us the wisdom, Jesus giving me life, and the Holy Spirit for leading us so we could train them up in the way they should go, giving them a solid foundation, so they can build on teaching their children to do likewise. We never built skyscrapers, made millions of dollars, or had much worldly goods, but we left them a good name so they would be grateful, kind, and loving—able to rise up and call us blessed!

Harris family with Harrison Wallis standing
in for his mother, Ruth Wallis

ABOUT THE AUTHOR

young mom

mom 2013

Frances L. Harris is a popular speaker at women's retreats, churches, and women's day fellowships. Her fervor for encouraging women in their spiritual, marital, and personal lives abounds in all she does. Whether she is hosting a local Bible study, an informal gathering at her home, or a chance meeting in town, Frances uses every opportunity to organize, teach, mentor, and inspire women to live up to their full potential. Her experience and wisdom comes from over fifty-six years of faithfully serving the same Lord and Savior, over fifty-five years of marriage to the same man, and raising eight children. She is an ardent servant who sets her affections on things above, not on things of this earth. Frances currently resides on her farm in Indiana enjoying life, friends and family.

"For the Lord is good; his steadfast love endures forever, and his faithfulness to all generations" (Psalm 100:5, ESV).

Mom and Dad, 1958

Mom and Dad, 2007